Beyond They/Them

Beyond They/ Them

20 INFLUENTIAL NONBINARY AND GENDER-DIVERSE PEOPLE YOU SHOULD KNOW

EM DICKSON

ILLUSTRATED BY
CAMERON MUKWA

Andrews McMeel
PUBLISHING®

FOR ANYONE WHO MIGHT SEE THEMSELVES
SOMEWHERE IN THESE PAGES, AND FOR MY
CHILD SELF WHO DIDN'T HAVE A BOOK LIKE THIS
AND SO DIDN'T HAVE THE WORDS. I HOPE THIS
HELPS YOU FIND YOUR WORDS.

—EM DICKSON

THERE IS INDEED NO ONE WAY TO BE TRANS. . . .
EXISTING OUTSIDE OF THE BINARY FOR ME IS FREEDOM.

—LAYSHIA CLARENDON

CONTENTS

AUTHOR'S NOTE

This author would like to acknowledge that identity labels can change, both due to personal self-awareness and growth and the evolutionary nature of language. At the time of writing, these are the words and the labels that the people we profile here use to describe themselves.

This author would also like to acknowledge that these individuals merely make up a small sample size of nonbinary and gender-diverse people from industries and generations around the world. Nonbinary people have always been here and can be found everywhere. To paraphrase Queen's University associate professor of gender and sexuality studies Dr. Lee Airton, gender diversity is not so much a new thing as it is a reemergence. To those who might disagree, I ask you, have you really not come across any nonbinary or gender-diverse people? Or did they just not have the words for it? Have you just not been paying attention?

A Note on Terms

The term *nonbinary* is used in this book both as an identity label and as an umbrella term for genders that exist outside the male/female binary. Nonbinary genders include but are not limited to genderfluid, genderqueer, and bigender. It's also important to note that there are many shared experiences across nonbinary and trans people, although not all nonbinary people identify as trans.

It is also important to acknowledge the existence of Indigenous gender identities, which might include third, fourth, or fifth genders. Among Indigenous North Americans, the term *two-spirit* is often used as an umbrella term for these gender identities, as well as additional queer and LGBTQIA+ identities. While many of these genders, such as the Diné náhleeh and dilbaa, the Native Hawaiian Māhū, and the Samoan fa'afafine and fa'afatama, have survived, there are likely countless other identities that have been lost due to Western imperialism and colonialism. To learn more about some of these identities and the issues they face, see "Discover More" on page 77.

INTRODUCTION

This book is a celebration.

    This book is about artists and activists and athletes and everything in between. This book tells a story of being who you are and chasing your dreams twenty times over (twenty-one, if you include this author).

This book is a demonstration.

    This book is about wonder, defiance, exhilaration, exploration. Exploring your gender as bravery. Courage in the face of pushback. Standing your ground when they ask you to step aside. Opening your arms wide to embrace who you are.

Exploring your gender can look like transitioning, either socially or medically; like defying preconceived gender roles; like shattering the glass box they put you in.

Exploring your gender can also look quiet. Like blue skies and sunset-pink clouds. Like crashing thunder and stormy seas. Like settling into your skin. Like joining the monster under your bed. Like carrying the weight of the sky. Like finally shrugging off that weight and letting it drift away.

Exploring your gender can look like finding yourself. Like being yourself. Like euphoria. Like joy. Like the sparkling of laughter. Like jubilation.

This book is a dedication. A dedication to all those who came before us and all who will come after. This book is a snapshot of the lives of twenty people. Just twenty people.

This book is a declaration. A declaration that your gender is a canvas only you can paint.

This book celebrates queer joy. This book celebrates gender euphoria. This book is a celebration.

This book is a celebration, a demonstration, an exploration, a jubilation, a dedication, a declaration.

This book is an invitation. Turn the page. Come on in. These doors will always remain open.

FILM & TV

ND STEVENSON

(HE / HIM)

- American cartoonist, animation producer, and television writer
- 2021 Annie Award nominee for Best Writing – TV/Media (*She-Ra and the Princesses of Power*, "Heart (Part 2)")
- 2021 Hugo Award nominee for Best Dramatic Presentation, Short Form (*She-Ra and the Princesses of Power*, "Heart (Part 2)")
- Coauthor of Eisner Award–winning series *Lumberjanes*
- Author and illustrator of graphic memoir *The Fire Never Goes Out: A Memoir in Pictures*
- Author and illustrator of *New York Times* bestselling and award-winning graphic novel *Nimona*

  - 2015 National Book Award finalist for Young People's Literature
  - 2015 Andre Norton Nebula Award® for Middle Grade and Young Adult Fiction finalist
  - 2016 Eisner Award winner

Did you know? ND Stevenson is married to fellow cartoonist and animation writer Molly Knox Ostertag, who's known for graphic novels like *The Witch Boy* trilogy and *The Girl From the Sea*, as well as for her work as an animation writer on the Disney Channel TV show *The Owl House.*

ND Stevenson (also known as Nate or Indy) was born in Columbia, South Carolina, on December 31, 1991, the third of five siblings in an evangelical Christian family. He was homeschooled until high school and often describes his childhood environment as conservative and religious, with rigid boundaries that made him feel very constrained. He explored such feelings through his art from an early age and went on to attend the Maryland Institute College of Art. While there, Stevenson began creating what would become his most famous work: *Nimona.*

Nimona was adapted into a hit animated film in 2023. The film was nominated for several awards,

including for an Academy Award for Best Animated Feature in 2024. *Nimona* was initially released as a webcomic before its publication as a graphic novel in 2015. The story of a young shapeshifter and her earnest but chaotic attempts to become the sidekick of a disillusioned fallen-knight-turned-supervillain, *Nimona* explores themes of acceptance, found family, and the fluidity of identity through deadpan humor and a medieval-futurist world setting. The character of Nimona has been long been celebrated as a metaphor for the trans, nonbinary, and gender-diverse experience. When asked about his own gender journey in relation to the creation of *Nimona*, Stevenson said:

I WAS MANY YEARS OUT FROM STARTING TO PUT ANY OF THE PIECES TOGETHER. SOME PEOPLE KNOW RIGHT AWAY, AND SOME PEOPLE LIKE ME NEED A LITTLE BIT MORE TIME TO SORT OF STUMBLE THROUGH AND END UP IN THE WRONG PLACE A FEW TIMES BEFORE YOU START REALLY PUTTING THINGS TOGETHER.

BUT I THINK FOR ME, FICTION AND CREATING STORIES HAS ALWAYS BEEN A WAY OF EXPLORING THOSE PARTS OF MYSELF BEFORE I MAY BE ABLE TO REALLY LOOK AT MYSELF WITH THAT CLEAR VISION.

In the graphic novel version of *Nimona*, the queer and trans themes are less explicit than they are subtext. That subtext was brought front and center in the film adaptation, which outright explored elements of the trans experience, such as animosity from strangers and clumsiness from friends who mean well in their attempts to understand.

Having his most famous character be an explosive shapeshifter who refuses to be anything but herself, in spite of being othered by society? A shapeshifter who inspires the people around her to be true to their own selves? A shapeshifter who fights back against the restraints that society tries to place around her? Nothing could be more fitting.

Stevenson came out as trans and nonbinary in 2020. He went on to declare himself transmasculine and bigender on 2021's International Transgender Day of Visibility. He shares snippets of his life and journey through comics on his Substack, *I'm Fine I'm Fine Just Understand*, where he first reintroduced himself as Nate in June 2022, though he continues to go by ND Stevenson

professionally. Aside from *Nimona*, he is also the creator and showrunner of the Daytime Emmy nominee and GLAAD Media Award–winning reboot of *She-Ra and the Princesses of Power*, an animated television series that ran for five seasons from 2018 to 2020.

Stevenson lives in Los Angeles with his wife, Molly Knox Ostertag.

REBECCA SUGAR

(SHE / THEY)

- American cartoonist, animator, screenwriter, producer, and singer-songwriter
- Writer and storyboard artist on the animated television series *Adventure Time* (Cartoon Network, 2010–2013)
- Creator of the groundbreaking and award-winning animated series *Steven Universe* (Cartoon Network, 2013–2019)

Did you know? Rebecca Sugar made history for Cartoon Network when she became the first woman to be the sole creator and showrunner of a series. This history was then crossed out, corrected, and made again when they came out as nonbinary, thus making them the first nonbinary person to achieve the same accomplishment.

Born into a Jewish family on July 9, 1987, and raised in Silver Spring, Maryland, Sugar showed an interest in art from an early age. They were recognized for their artistic excellence throughout high school, writing a comic strip for the school newspaper while simultaneously attending art classes through the Montgomery County Public Schools Visual Art Center (VAC) Program, receiving such honors as a nomination for the US Presidential Scholar in the Arts. Sugar's younger brother, Steven, the namesake for the title character in *Steven Universe*, also attended the VAC program and went on to work as a background designer on the show.

Steven Universe was inspired in many ways by the fairy tales and golden age of Disney movies that Sugar grew up with, and the show feels almost like a fairy tale itself—with its whimsy and romance—even as it tackles traumas and the complexity of coming of age. However, the show moves beyond classic fairy tales with its nuanced emotional resonance and intrinsic celebration of queer positivity and joy. At San Diego Comic-Con 2016, Sugar made headlines when she came out as bisexual in response to an audience question surrounding the inspiration for the centering of women's empowerment and LGBTQIA+ themes in *Steven Universe*. Sugar went on to say:

THESE THEMES HAVE SO MUCH TO DO WITH WHO YOU ARE. THERE'S AN IDEA THAT . . . THESE ARE THEMES THAT SHOULD NOT BE SHARED WITH KIDS, BUT EVERYONE SHARES STORIES ABOUT LOVE AND ATTRACTION WITH KIDS. SO MANY STORIES FOR KIDS ARE ABOUT LOVE, AND IT REALLY MAKES A DIFFERENCE TO HEAR STORIES ABOUT HOW SOMEONE LIKE YOU CAN BE LOVED. AND IF YOU DON'T HEAR THOSE STORIES, IT WILL CHANGE WHO YOU ARE. IT'S VERY IMPORTANT TO ME THAT WE SPEAK TO KIDS ABOUT CONSENT, THAT WE SPEAK TO KIDS ABOUT IDENTITY, THAT WE SPEAK TO KIDS ABOUT SO MUCH. I WANT TO FEEL LIKE I EXIST, AND I WANT EVERYONE ELSE WHO WANTS TO FEEL THAT WAY TO FEEL THAT WAY, TOO.

In the years since, Sugar has also spoken about exploring her own identity as a nonbinary woman through the Gems, a group of extraterrestrial characters in *Steven Universe*. In a July 2018 interview with NPR, Sugar said:

ONE OF THE THINGS THAT'S REALLY IMPORTANT TO ME ABOUT THE SHOW IS THAT THE GEMS ARE ALL NONBINARY WOMEN. THEY'RE VERY SPECIFIC, AND THEY'RE COMING FROM A WORLD WHERE THEY DON'T REALLY HAVE THE FRAME OF REFERENCE. THEY'RE CODED FEMALE, WHICH IS VERY IMPORTANT. . . . I WAS REALLY EXCITED BECAUSE I FELT LIKE I HAD NOT SEEN THIS. TO MAKE A SHOW ABOUT A YOUNG BOY WHO WAS LOOKING UP TO THESE FEMALE-CODED CHARACTERS. . . . THEY APPEAR TO BE FEMALE, [BUT] THEY'RE A LITTLE MORE REPRESENTATIVE OF NONBINARY WOMEN.

THEY WOULDN'T THINK OF THEMSELVES AS WOMEN, BUT THEY'RE FINE WITH BEING INTERPRETED THAT WAY AMONGST HUMANS. AND I AM ALSO A NONBINARY WOMAN, WHICH [HAS] BEEN REALLY GREAT TO EXPRESS MYSELF THROUGH THESE CHARACTERS, BECAUSE IT'S VERY MUCH HOW I HAVE FELT THROUGHOUT MY LIFE.

Between Sugar's work on both *Steven Universe* and *Adventure Time*, they have earned several Primetime Emmy Award nominations and three Annie Award nominations. They also won the 2019 GLAAD Media Award for Outstanding Kids & Family Programming for *Steven Universe*. Sugar now lives in California with their spouse, fellow animator and frequent collaborator Ian Jones-Quartey. The two married in December 2019, after having been in a relationship for twelve years.

VICO ORTIZ

(THEY / THEM · ELLE / LE / E)

- Puerto Rican actor, voice actor, drag king (known as Vico Suave), and activist
- Gold Derby TV Awards nominee—Best Comedy Supporting Actor (2022)

Did you know? Vico Ortiz is not exactly well-known for being on Puerto Rico's national fencing team from age thirteen to seventeen, but this did prepare them well for the stunt work involved in their portrayal of nonbinary pirate Jim in the hit HBO show *Our Flag Means Death*.

Vico Ortiz was born on October 10, 1991, and grew up in a theater family in San Juan, Puerto Rico. Ortiz always knew they wanted to be an actor. After graduating high school and retiring from the Puerto Rican national fencing team at age seventeen, Ortiz moved to Los Angeles to attend the American Academy of Dramatic Arts and pursue acting full-time.

Ortiz has consistently advocated for incorporating their own genderfluid and nonbinary identity into their characters and has actively worked toward greater gender-diverse representation on-screen. While Ortiz has had guest spots on popular shows like *The Fosters* and *Criminal Minds*, they are best known as nonbinary pirate Jim Jimenez in the hit HBO ensemble series *Our Flag Means Death* (2022–2023). The show, a fictionalized love story between historical figures Blackbeard and gentleman pirate Stede Bonnet, delves into the misadventures of the emotionally aware crew on a journey of queerness, found family, and self-acceptance. Despite a lack of marketing for the first season, the period romantic comedy quickly became a sleeper hit celebrated for its centering of BIPOC and queer identities amid a slew of hijinks

on the high seas. As Jim Jimenez, Ortiz showed off their fencing background in addition to their superior knife-wielding skills. With the support of a writers' room with no fewer than three gender-diverse people, the character of Jim uses *they/them* pronouns and is immediately accepted by the rest of the crew. On portraying Jim, Ortiz told *PinkNews*:

> IT FELT LIKE I WAS RECLAIMING SOME OF OUR STORIES. UNFORTUNATELY, THROUGHOUT HISTORY A LOT OF THE TRANS, NONBINARY, [AND] QUEER STORIES TRY TO TALK ABOUT THE PERSON AS MUCH AS POSSIBLE WITHOUT ACKNOWLEDGING THAT THEY'RE QUEER. WHEN I READ FOR THE PART AND GOT TO INTERPRET JIM, IT WAS LIKE, OH YEAH, I GET TO ACTUALLY FEARLESSLY EMBODY THIS JOURNEY OF SOMEONE WHO [GETS TO EXPLORE] THEIR IDENTITY.

In looking back at their own gender-exploration journey, Ortiz notes that they have always been drawn to men who are in touch with their femininity. Their drag king persona, Vico Suave, is inspired by men like Ricky Martin, Freddie Mercury, and Bad Bunny and by Latine and American cultures. Ortiz also performs in the boy band the Backstreet Butches, under a second drag persona named AJ. They have described their gender identity as both nonbinary and genderfluid, comparing the experience to a waterbed: "constantly moving, but in a fun way."

A piece of *Our Flag Means Death* fan art depicting Roach, the ship's cook and de facto surgeon, performing top surgery on the character of Jim Jimenez inspired Ortiz to undergo the procedure themself. It provided an avenue through which Ortiz could see themself.

As an activist, Ortiz stands up for Puerto Rican voting rights and for gender inclusivity within the gendered language of Spanish, among other causes related to social justice like antiracism and trans rights. Ortiz declared to *TODAY*, "I'm not just fighting for me. I'm fighting for the freedom of all of us. My queerness has given me a lens to see how things are affecting all of us of every walk of life."

In addition to their on-screen work, Ortiz has also voiced several audiobooks written by gender-diverse authors, such as the young adult novels *Bianca Torre Is Afraid of Everything* by Justine Pucella Winans and *The Wicked Bargain* by Gabe Cole Novoa. They also served as one of many narrators in the audiobook edition of young adult anthology *Transmogrify!: 14 Fantastical Tales of Trans Magic*, edited by g. haron davis, and as one of two narrators for the audiobook of young adult novel *Venom & Vow* by Anna-Marie McLemore and Elliott McLemore.

BOOKS & POETRY

MAIA KOBABE

(E / EM / EIR)

- American author/illustrator
- 2016 Ignatz Award nominee—Promising New Talent (*Tom O'Bedlam*)
- 2019 Ignatz Award nominee—Outstanding Graphic Novel (*Gender Queer: A Memoir*)
- 2020 American Library Association's Alex Award winner (*Gender Queer: A Memoir*)
- 2020 YALSA Great Graphic Novels for Teens (*Gender Queer: A Memoir*)
- 2020 Stonewall Book Awards—Israel Fishman Non-Fiction Honor Book (*Gender Queer: A Memoir*)

Did you know? Kobabe's pronouns, *e/em/eir*, are known as Spivak pronouns. This set of pronouns was named for American mathematician Michael Spivak, who popularized their use (though capitalized *E/Em/Eir*) in his 1982 book, *The Joy of TeX*. However, variations on an epicene pronoun that uses *e*, *ey*, or *em* have independently emerged several times both before and after Spivak's publication, with the earliest recorded (*e/es/em*) in an 1890 editorial by James Rogers. The most popular variations seem to be *ey/em/eir*, coined by Christine Elverson in 1975, and Spivak's *e/em/eir*.

Maia Kobabe was born in 1989 and grew up in a rustic community in the Bay Area, California, where eir parents spent time carving beads, weaving, and sewing. From a young age, Kobabe attended Waldorf schools, where there was a heavy emphasis on handcrafts and the arts, but that suited em just fine. Diagnosed with dyslexia, e struggled to read until the age of eleven but loved comics, fantasy novels, and imagining emself in other worlds. Without TV and with little to no internet, Kobabe had the freedom to wander outdoors in every direction, feeling at home in catching frogs or picking berries—if not quite at home in eir own body.

Nonbinary, queer, bi, and asexual (though it would be years before e had the words for any of it), Kobabe struggled to see emself in the stories e consumed. How can you imagine yourself as something you've never seen? Still, Kobabe continued to explore themes of identity in eir own work. E came out as bisexual in high school, but it wasn't until 2016 that e started to tentatively come out as nonbinary, eventually exploring this chronicle of self-discovery through eir first full-length book, *Gender Queer: A Memoir*, which was published in May 2019 to great acclaim.

Gender Queer began as a way for Kobabe to explain eir nonbinary and asexual identity to eir well-meaning yet confused friends and family, but it soon became more than a diaristic chronicle of self-discovery—it became a lifeline for questioning young people everywhere who, like Kobabe, have always yearned for a book like this. There is a gentle earnestness to *Gender Queer*, even as Kobabe depicts a bewildering struggle for clarity and belonging throughout eir adolescence. In addition to receiving the American Library Association's Alex Award and a Stonewall Book Award Honor in 2020, *Gender Queer* has been recognized across the country for its excellence.

The recognition that Kobabe likely wishes *Gender Queer* would stop receiving? That of the No. 1 banned book in the United States. *Gender Queer* has received this so-called honor every year since 2021, when it began receiving pushback from conservative politicians and groups like Moms for Liberty, who first demanded its removal from schools and libraries in the run up to the fall US midterm election.

In a May 2022 interview with *The New York Times*, Kobabe had this to say: "When you remove those books from the shelf or you challenge them publicly in a community, what you're saying to any young person who identified with that narrative is, 'We don't want your story here.'"

Kobabe has battled fears surrounding queer visibility, which e explored in *Gender Queer.*

Since the initial outpouring of national headlines, Kobabe has stood up for eir work and queer youth everywhere, advocating heavily for teachers and librarians. Kobabe worked in libraries for more than ten years before becoming a full-time freelancer and teaching comics classes to young people at various intervals. Eir short comics have been published online by *The Nib* and *The New Yorker* and in print anthologies like *The Secret Loves of Geeks* and *Be Gay, Do Comics*. Kobabe continues to explore themes of gender, queerness, and identity in eir work.

I WISH I DIDN'T FEAR THAT MY IDENTITY IS TOO POLITICAL FOR A CLASSROOM. . . . I WONDER IF ANY OF THESE KIDS ARE TRANS OR NONBINARY, BUT DON'T HAVE WORDS FOR IT YET? HOW MANY OF THEM HAVE NEVER SEEN A NONBINARY ADULT? IS MY SILENCE ACTUALLY A DISSERVICE TO ALL OF THEM? . . . EVERY TIME I FAIL TO GIVE MY PRONOUNS I FEEL LIKE A COWARD.

SARAH GAILEY
(THEY / THEM)

- American author
- 2017 John W. Campbell Award finalist—Best New Writer
- 2017 Nebula Award® finalist—Best Novella (*River of Teeth*)
- 2018 Hugo Award finalist—Best Novella (*River of Teeth*)
- 2018 Locus Award finalist—Novella (*River of Teeth*)
- 2018 Hugo Award winner—Best Fan Writer
- 2019 Hugo Award finalist—Best Short Story ("STET")
- 2019 Locus Award finalist—Short Story ("STET")
- 2020 Hugo Award finalist—Best Novelette (*Away With the Wolves*)
- 2020 Locus Award finalist—First Novel (*Magic for Liars*)
- 2021 Hugo Award finalist—Best Novella (*Upright Women Wanted*)
- 2021 Locus Award finalist—Novella (*Upright Women Wanted*)

Did you know? Sarah Gailey's award-winning novella *River of Teeth* was inspired by the American Hippo bill of the early twentieth century, when the United States actually considered creating an industry around importing hippos as a meat product and raising them akin to cows. Sure, bring over the most dangerous megafauna in Africa. That wouldn't be a disaster or anything.

Sarah Gailey was born on February 2, 1990, in Fremont, California. Their mother worked at a bookstore, which helped spark their lifelong love of reading and especially genre fiction. They went on to study theater at the American Academy of Dramatic Arts. From there, they managed a theater company and later worked as a temp at a research firm. After feeling like they were floundering, Gailey began writing. They first started publishing genre work online in 2015, but their breakout work came with the alternate-history novella *River of Teeth* in 2017, the opener to their American Hippo duology. *River of Teeth* was the first of many works by Gailey to be nominated for the Hugo, Nebula, and Locus Awards, some of the premier awards for science fiction or fantasy works.

Gailey's fiction explores messy, complex characters and themes of queerness and identity through the lens

of magic and fantasy, whether in an alternate history setting or a futuristic Wild West. Their debut novel, *Magic for Liars*, a murder mystery set at a magical boarding school, features characters who go through iterations of trying on different identities to see what fits. Gailey's first young adult book, *When We Were Magic*, leans into the joy of finding oneself in community, all in the fallout of a magical disaster and told in a voice laced with dark humor.

When Gailey was young, they had never considered that queer people could have happy endings—all they saw were queer-coded villains and queer stories that ended in tragedy. They're helping to change that. In a June 2019 interview with *Kirkus Reviews*, Gailey noted:

AS A QUEER PERSON, I WANT TO BUILD BOOKS THAT HAVE WORLDS WHERE QUEERNESS IS ALLOWED AND IT'S PART OF PEOPLE'S COMMUNITIES. I DON'T WANT TO KEEP ON HAVING THOSE CONVERSATIONS OF, LIKE, "WHY DO YOU USE THEY / THEM PRONOUNS? WHAT DOES THAT MEAN?" I JUST WANT TO READ A WORLD WHERE THEY / THEM PRONOUNS EXIST AND IT'S FINE.

Gailey has published speculative fiction, short stories, and essays, with their shorter works and essays showcased online or in print through outlets such as *The Boston Globe*, Mashable, Reactor, *VICE*, and *The Atlantic*. Gailey has lived and worked in Los Angeles since 2019.

DR. JOSHUA WHITEHEAD

(HE / HIM)

. Canadian First Nations storyteller and scholar

. Two-spirit/Indigiqueer, Oji-nêhiyaw member of Peguis First Nation (Treaty 1/Manitoba)

. 2019 Lambda Literary Award for Gay Fiction (*Jonny Appleseed*)

. 2021 Lambda Literary Award for LGBTQ Anthology (*Love After the End: An Anthology of Two-Spirit and Indigiqueer Speculative Fiction*)

Did you know? Joshua Whitehead's debut publication, *full-metal indigiqueer*, an experimental poetry collection-meets-cyberpunk odyssey, was nominated for the 2018 Lambda Literary Award for Transgender Poetry. In a stunningly expressive letter, Whitehead withdrew his work from consideration, citing the category in question as a misrepresentation of his identity as a two-spirit—not transgender—person. He would go on to win multiple Lambda Literary Awards for later works.

Joshua Whitehead was born on January 5, 1989, to a trucker father and a mother who worked at a shelter for Indigenous women. Raised in Selkirk, Manitoba, he spent much of his summers in Peguis First Nation with his maternal grandmother and extended family. Like many writers, Whitehead spent a lot of time at the library. He was an avid reader, and childhood favorites included C. S. Lewis's *Chronicles of Narnia*, J. R. R. Tolkien's *Lord of the Rings*, Ursula K. Le Guin's Earthsea Cycle, and Brian Jacques's *Redwall*. It wasn't until he read Toni Morrison's *Beloved* in a course at the University of Winnipeg that something clicked for him. To *Maclean's*, a Canadian magazine, Whitehead credited Morrison as "teaching me how not to write white" through "all of her work—the vernacular use, the morality, the use of temporality to mix past, present, and future."

For Whitehead, his Indigeneity and queerness are intrinsically linked, braided together, which he has delved into as a scholar of Indigenous languages and cultures with a focus on gender and sexuality. His creative work is a natural extension and reflection of his scholarly pursuits, bringing two-spirit/Indigiqueer representation to the forefront. In a 2017 interview with CBC Radio, Whitehead declared, "We are not a was. We are not this kind of mythic kind of romantic idea of what two-spirited people are or what they were."

Whitehead's work celebrates the resurgence of Indigiqueer identity, a reclamation as much as a resistance against settler colonialism. His debut publication, *full-metal indigiqueer*, builds toward an Indigiqueer future, not so much bending boundaries as shattering them between genres and conventions, dipping and weaving between clashes with historical and contemporary literary and pop culture figures from Shakespeare to RuPaul. He brings Indigiqueerness into the here and now by directly confronting settler colonialism through literary and pop culture references, which also serve as a touchstone and entryway for readers who might not be as familiar with Indigiqueer identities and storytelling—even as Indigiqueer readers remain centered.

His debut novel, *Jonny Appleseed*, interrogates similar themes through the story of a young two-spirit/Indigiqueer who struggles to fit the pieces of himself together as he returns home to his reserve for his stepfather's funeral. Told with a sparkling vividity, *Jonny Appleseed* was recognized by several organizations for its excellence, and it won the Lambda Literary Award for Gay Fiction and was long-listed for many other awards.

Whitehead's further work, whether prose, verse, or a blend of the two, continues to explore such themes as Indigeneity, queerness, mental health, grief, healing, and the connection of the body to the earth. He served as editor for the Lambda Literary Award–winning work *Love After the End: An Anthology of Two-Spirit and Indigiqueer Speculative Fiction*, a series of subversive stories that explores many of the same themes. The particular blend of prose and verse in *Making Love with the Land*, Whitehead's first full-length work of creative nonfiction, draws from oral storytelling traditions in an almost stream-of-consciousness narrative form that he calls "biostory." To *Electric Literature*, Whitehead described biostory as a deconstruction of genre, a "way to pay homage to the oral stories of the peoples I come from as well as fully embedded within my physical body but also the layered textures of our bodies of water, land, and text too."

Whitehead is an assistant professor at the University of Calgary on Treaty 7 territory, where he earned a PhD in Indigenous literatures and cultures, with a focus on gender and sexuality. The groundbreaking nature of his work might best be summed up by his declaration: "If I was to be decolonial on the land, I needed to do it on the page too."

MUSIC

SAM SMITH

(THEY / THEM)

- English singer-songwriter
- 2015 Billboard Music Awards—thirteen nominations, three wins:

  - Top New Artist
  - Top Male Artist
  - Top Radio Songs Artist

- 2016 Academy Award Winner—Best Original Song ("Writing's on the Wall")
- 2016 Golden Globe Award Winner—Best Original Song ("Writing's on the Wall")
- BRIT Awards—fourteen nominations, four wins:

  - 2014 Critics' Choice Award
  - 2015 British Breakthrough Act Award
  - 2015 Global Success Award
  - 2023 BRIT Billion Award

- Grammy Awards—seven nominations, five wins:

  - 2015 Best New Artist
  - 2015 Best Pop Vocal Album (*In the Lonely Hour*)
  - 2015 Record of the Year ("Stay with Me" [Darkchild Version])
  - 2015 Song of the Year ("Stay with Me" [Darkchild Version])
  - 2023 Best Pop Duo/Group Performance ("Unholy," with Kim Petras)

Did you know? Sam Smith became the first openly nonbinary solo artist to reach No. 1 on the Billboard Hot 100™ with "Unholy," sung with Kim Petras, who became the first openly transgender solo artist to achieve the same honor. "Unholy" went on to win the 2023 Grammy Award for Best Pop Duo/Group Performance, with Smith the first openly nonbinary artist and Petras the first openly transgender artist to win a Grammy.

Sam Smith was born on May 19, 1992, and raised in rural Cambridgeshire, England. Throughout their youth, they dabbled with gender expression and the blurring of traditional gender roles, though they also struggled with body image due to bullying. In a March 2019 interview on Jameela Jamil's Instagram show, *I Weigh Interviews*, Smith spoke about their childhood, from when they first came out as gay at age ten to when they stopped wearing "male" clothing at age sixteen and often wore makeup to school. They spoke, too, about undergoing liposuction at age twelve after they began developing breasts due to an excess of the hormone estrogen in their chest—an example of gender-affirming medical care for someone who, at the time, was assumed to be cis.

Smith was always a singer, performing with jazz bands and in youth choirs and musical theatre. Their bold powerhouse voice is known for its range, soaring from a rich baritone to a high, clear tenor.

Guess who? Which of the following group of artists has Smith cited as sources of musical inspiration and empowerment?

a. Adele, Amy Winehouse, Mary J. Blige, and Lady Gaga

b. Whitney Houston, Aretha Franklin, George Michael, and Elton John

c. Chaka Khan, Robyn, Beyoncé, and Brandy

d. Christina Aguilera, Mariah Carey, and Britney Spears

e. All of the above

Smith first became known for features on Disclosure's song "Latch" and Naughty Boy's song "La La La," both of which did very well, peaking at No. 11 and No. 1, respectively, on the UK Singles Chart.

After releasing the EP *Nirvana* in 2013, they released their first studio album, *In the Lonely Hour*, on May 26, 2014, which catapulted them to pop stardom. Smith won four Grammy Awards in 2015, including Best New Artist and Record of the Year for their breakout song, "Stay With Me (Darkchild Version)." They have been nominated for seven Grammys, winning five. Their song "Writing's on the Wall," written with Jimmy Napes for the 2015 James Bond film *Spectre*, won an Academy Award and a Golden Globe Award, both for Best Original Song. Smith has also been nominated for countless BRIT Awards, Billboard Music Awards, American Music Awards, and many others, and has won several.

After first publicly coming out as gay in 2014 and genderqueer in 2017, and having dropped comments here and there about their journey of gender exploration, in September 2019, Smith officially came out as nonbinary, announcing their pronouns as *they/them*. In the initial online post, Smith declared, "After a lifetime of being at war with my gender I've decided to embrace myself for who I am, inside and out." Smith has reflected on their journey since coming out, saying in January 2023 that "since changing my pronouns, it felt like coming home. I wish I knew what the words were when I was in school, because I would've identified as that in school. Because it is who I am and it's who I've always been."

Smith's music videos in recent years have been celebrations of queerness, centering people of various gender identities and presentations wearing everything from suits to corsets and ruffled dresses—Smith included. Despite a far-right backlash rooted in queerphobia, femmephobia, and fatphobia, Smith continues to make unabashedly queer art. They refuse to let such backlash overshadow their queer joy.

Answer: e. All of the above

DEMI LOVATO
(THEY / SHE)

- American singer, songwriter, actor, and activist

- Teen Choice Awards: multiple nominations and wins, including

    o 2009 Choice Music: Tour ("Summer Tour 2009" [with David Archuleta])
    o 2011 Acuvue Inspire Award
    o 2011 Choice Song of the Summer ("Skyscraper")
    o 2012 Choice Summer Female Music Star
    o 2013 Choice Female Artist
    o 2014 Choice Summer Music Star: Female
    o 2015 Choice Music: Female Artist

- People's Choice Awards: multiple nominations and wins, including

    o 2012 Favorite Pop Artist
    o 2013 Favorite Celebrity Judge *(The X Factor [US])*
    o 2014 Favorite Female Artist

- Two-time Grammy nominee

    o 2016 Best Pop Vocal Album (*Confident*)
    o 2019 Best Pop Duo/Group Performance ("Fall in Line" [with Christina Aguilera])

Did you know? Demi Lovato is a purple belt in the sport of Brazilian jiujitsu. They began training in the martial art in 2016.

Demetria "Demi" Lovato was born on August 20, 1992, in Albuquerque, New Mexico, before being raised in Dallas, Texas, by their mother after their parents' divorce in 1994. Interested in performing from an early age, she began playing the piano at age seven and the guitar at age ten, which is when she also began taking dancing and acting lessons. Around the same time, Lovato got their start on *Barney & Friends*, where they spent the next two years as a cast member from age ten to twelve alongside future Disney Channel costar Selena Gomez.

Lovato debuted on Disney Channel at age fifteen in 2007 as a lead in the short comedy series *As the Bell Rings*, which often aired during the commercial breaks of longer shows. Lovato shot to stardom the following year for their lead role in *Camp Rock* (2008) alongside the Jonas Brothers. Lovato's debut single from the film, "This Is Me," reached No. 9 on the US Billboard Hot 100 chart, leading her to sign with Hollywood Records (and later signing with Island Records). Lovato, who quickly became known for their eager smile and powerhouse vocal abilities, released their debut studio album, *Don't Forget*, in 2008.

At the time of writing, Lovato has released eight studio albums, and their vocals were also featured on *No Promises* by Cheat Codes, which was released in 2017 to commercial acclaim. Lovato has received hundreds of nominations for their work, winning People's Choice Awards, Teen Choice Awards, and countless others over the course of their career

Lovato continued to appear on television after parting with Disney Channel, though she has primarily

Do you know all these hit songs by Demi Lovato?

- "Get Back" (*Don't Forget*, 2008)

- "Here We Go Again" (*Here We Go Again*, 2009)

- "Skyscraper" (*Unbroken*, 2011)

- "Give Your Heart a Break" (*Unbroken*, 2011)

- "Heart Attack" (*Demi*, 2013)

- "Cool for the Summer" (*Confident*, 2015)

- "Sorry Not Sorry" (*Tell Me You Love Me*, 2017)

been featured as a guest or a judge on shows like *The X Factor*, *The Voice*, and *Project Runway*. She did have a recurring role in season 5 of *Glee* in 2013, where she played a brief girlfriend of fan-favorite character Santana (Naya Rivera). In a tribute to the late Rivera in 2020, Lovato posted on Instagram that she'll "forever cherish the opportunity to play your girlfriend on *Glee*. The character you played was groundbreaking for tons of closeted queer girls (like me at the time)." This was the first time that Lovato publicly claimed the label *queer*, later coming out as pansexual and sexually fluid in a March 2021 interview. That May, Lovato revealed the "revelation that I identify as nonbinary" in the first episode of their new podcast, *4D with Demi Lovato*. They went on to say:

I'LL BE OFFICIALLY CHANGING MY PRONOUNS TO THEY / THEM. I FEEL THAT THIS BEST REPRESENTS THE FLUIDITY I FEEL IN MY GENDER EXPRESSION AND ALLOWS ME TO FEEL MOST AUTHENTIC AND TRUE TO THE PERSON I BOTH KNOW I AM AND AM STILL DISCOVERING.

In an August 2022 interview, Lovato readopted the use of *she/her* pronouns in addition to *they/them*, stating that they'd recently been feeling more feminine. The following June, Lovato explained that she'd grown exhausted with having to constantly explain herself and her gender identity, so she readopted *she/her* pronouns to sidestep that process.

Lovato spoke further about their discomfort with various spaces, such as government forms and public bathrooms, that require you to choose between two binary genders. Lovato spoke, too, of the need for more gender-neutral spaces, adding that they would "feel more comfortable in a genderless bathroom." The most important thing for Lovato in regard to publicly discussing their gender journey? "It will be worth it as long as there are people who tell me that I am an inspiration to them or that I have helped them learn more about themselves and feel more comfortable in their skin."

Lovato has been honored for their efforts to raise awareness for mental health issues and their efforts to combat bullying, as well as their activism on behalf of LGBTQIA+ rights. She has also spoken out against racial injustice, police brutality, and gun violence for several years. Lovato's philanthropic work and activism have included partnerships with the Human Rights Campaign, March for Our Lives, Global Citizen, and Save the Children, and advocating for gun reform, LGBTQIA+ rights, and climate justice, among other causes.

After the death of her father, with whom she had a strained relationship, she founded the Lovato Treatment Scholarship Program, which has funded the treatment costs of mentally ill patients since 2013. Lovato has been open about their own struggles with mental health and substance abuse and continues to advocate and raise awareness to this day.

JANELLE MONÁE

(THEY / SHE)

- American singer, songwriter, rapper, and actor
- Ten-time Grammy Award nominee:

  - 2008 Best Urban/Alternative Performance ("Many Moons")
  - 2011 Best Contemporary R&B Album (*The ArchAndroid*)
  - 2011 Best Urban/Alternative Performance ("Tightrope")
  - 2012 Record of the Year ("We Are Young" [with fun.])
  - 2012 Best Pop Duo/Group Performance ("We Are Young" [with fun.])
  - 2012 Album of the Year (*Some Nights* [with fun.])
  - 2019 Best Music Video ("PYNK")
  - 2019 Album of the Year (*Dirty Computer*)
  - 2024 Best Progressive R&B Album (*The Age of Pleasure*)
  - 2024 Album of the Year (*The Age of Pleasure*)

- 2012 Grammy Award—Song of the Year ("We Are Young" [with fun.])
- 2014 NAACP Image Award—Outstanding Music Video ("Q.U.E.E.N." [feat. Erykah Badu])
- 2014 Variety Breakthrough of the Year Award—Music
- 2019 GLAAD Media Award—Outstanding Music Artist (*Dirty Computer)*
- 2023 Critics Choice Award—Best Acting Ensemble (*Glass Onion: A Knives Out Mystery*)

Did you know? Janelle Monáe has cited Dorothy Gale from *The Wizard of Oz* as a musical inspiration for them—fitting for a performing artist from Kansas!

Janelle Monáe was born on December 1, 1985, in Kansas City, Kansas, and raised in the working-class community of Quindaro by parents employed in the service industry. Surrounded by a large extended family of church performers and musicians, Monáe quickly joined the fray, learning to sing at a local church and performing in talent showcases whenever possible. As a teenager, they were part of a young playwrights program, and after high school they went on to study musical theater at the American Musical and Dramatic Academy in New York City. With her schooling partially funded

by her congregation back home, Monáe felt isolated from primarily white and privileged classmates. After a year and a half of listening to her best friend gush over the Black community she'd found at school in Atlanta, Monáe moved down south into a boardinghouse directly across the street from Atlanta's four historically Black colleges and universities (HBCUs), where she began writing and performing her own music around campus.

Monáe was featured on OutKast's 2006 album, and they soon followed up with their own singles. Monae's initial releases here were from the point of view of their alter ego, Cindi Mayweather, an android from the year 2719 whose story is chronicled in a seven-part conceptual series. Often likened to Neo-Afrofuturism and inspired by Fritz Lang's 1927 classic futuristic film *Metropolis*, this series wowed both critically and commercially for its dazzling radicality.

Cindi Mayweather represents the "Other," which feels very much like a queer allegory—with *The New York Times* noting in a 2018 feature that "Mayweather was a proxy for all the things about Monáe that made others uncomfortable, like her androgyny, her opaque sexual identity, her gender fluidity—her defiance of easy categorization."

With a dynamic voice and mesmerizing stage presence, Monáe has been compared to performers across a wide spectrum that includes Judy Garland, Buddy Holly, James Brown, Prince, Lauryn Hill, and Corinne Bailey Rae. Her musical influences include jazz, rap, funk, and psychedelic soul, while her style influences include Grace Jones, Katharine Hepburn, and silent film actress Josephine Baker. Monáe rocks a lot of tuxedos and enjoys playing with a style that redefines clothing as without gender.

With their genre-defying music and gender-defying style, Monáe was celebrated as a queer icon before they ever publicly came out as pansexual in 2018 on the cover of *Rolling Stone* magazine. After much speculation about their gender identity, partially kickstarted from their retweet of the *Steven Universe* meme "*Are you a boy or a girl?*" "*I'm an experience!*" in January 2020, Monáe officially came out as nonbinary on an April 2022 episode of *Red Table Talk*:

I'M NONBINARY, SO I JUST DON'T SEE MYSELF AS A WOMAN, SOLELY. I FEEL ALL OF MY ENERGY. I FEEL LIKE GOD IS SO MUCH BIGGER THAN THE HE OR THE SHE. IF I AM FROM GOD, I AM EVERYTHING. BUT I WILL ALWAYS, ALWAYS STAND WITH WOMEN. I WILL ALWAYS STAND WITH BLACK WOMEN. BUT I JUST SEE EVERYTHING BEYOND THE BINARY.

As an actor, Monáe first appeared on-screen in 2016 as Teresa in *Moonlight* before starring as Mary Jackson in *Hidden Figures* that same year. She also had supporting roles in the 2019 films *Harriet* and the live-action *Lady and the Tramp*. Monáe portrayed identical twins Cassandra and Helen Brand in *Glass Onion: A Knives Out Mystery* to great acclaim.

CRIS DERKSEN

(SHE / HER)

. Two-spirit Cree cellist and composer

. 2016 JUNO Award nominee—Instrumental Album of the Year (*Orchestral Powwow*)

. 2017 Indigenous Music Awards nominee—Best Instrumental Album (*Orchestral Powwow*)

Did you know? In 2019, Cris Derksen composed the grand finale for the Luminato Festival in Toronto, performed by more than two hundred singers! The event, Maada'ookii Songlines, involved physical elements as part of the performance, such as the youngest performers carrying little lights that created the illusion of fireflies after the sun went down mid-show.

Cris Derksen was trained in classical music from an early age, experimenting with the piano, flute, saxophone, and double-bass before focusing on cello in high school. Born in 1981 and raised on the North Tallcree reserve in Northern Alberta, Canada (Treaty 8), Derksen is descended from a line of Cree chiefs on her father's side and Mennonite homesteaders on her mother's. Derksen attended a performing arts high school in Edmonton, and went on to receive a bachelor of music in cello performance at the University of British Columbia, where she was the principal cellist of the UBC Symphony Orchestra.

After graduating from university, Derksen began performing with Inuk throat singer Tanya Tagaq and quickly became recognized for a unique sound that blends classical music with the music of her Indigenous heritage. After performing internationally with Tagaq for three years, Derksen embarked on her solo career. In a 2015 interview with *Musicworks* magazine, she spoke candidly of her artistry:

CONTEMPORARY AND TRADITIONAL HAVE ALWAYS BEEN IN MY BRAIN—INCORPORATING THE TRADITIONS OF MY ABORIGINAL HERITAGE INTO THE NEW CONTEMPORARY SCHOOLS THAT I PLAY IN. IT'S ALMOST LIKE BEING A JEWELER MAKING A BRACELET— YOU'RE GOING TO PICK OUT THE STONES THAT SPEAK TO YOU. SO I TAKE ALL THESE INFLUENCES AND CREATE THE BRACELET THAT ONLY I CAN MAKE, BECAUSE IT'S MY PERCEPTION OF THE WORLD.

Derksen's third studio album, *Orchestral Powwow*, a veritable master class of this symphonic folk fusion of the classical, Indigenous, and modern electronic, was nominated for a JUNO Award. Derksen's live performances absolutely stagger—she makes the cello croon like a living being, treating the bow, strings, and body with tenderness and with a percussive element that calls back to folk traditions, adding layers with loop pedals until she is a soaring one-person symphony.

An internationally renowned cellist, Derksen has performed both across Canada and around the world. She made her Carnegie Hall debut on March 6, 2024, with the Orchestre Métropolitain de Montréal. In addition to her performance work, Derksen has composed for symphonies and chamber orchestras and for choral groups, dance troupes, theater productions, documentaries, and the CBC.

CBC Radio interviewed Derksen and several queer Indigenous artists for a feature in February 2024. She spoke of one of her more personal works, "Top Shelf," a song that she cowrote with her partner, Rebecca Benson. Derksen described "Top Shelf" as a "two-spirit love song." In the same interview, Derksen said she hopes that her work "can help connect Indigenous and queer creators with the rest of the classical music community."

SPORTS

QUINN

(THEY / THEM)

- Canadian professional soccer player

  - Seattle Reign FC (2019–)
  - 2022 NWSL Shield

- Canada Women's National Team midfielder
- 2016 and 2021 Olympic Games medalist
- 2022 Forbes 30 Under 30—Sports
- Nike Athlete
- Athlete Ally Action Award (2021)
- Playing for Pride supporter
- See Them, Be Them mentor

Did you know? Quinn uses a mononym—one name to encompass both their first name and surname.

Quinn was born on August 11, 1995, into a sports family in Toronto, Ontario. Both of their parents were college athletes—their mother had played basketball, and their father had played rugby. Growing up, Quinn, along with their three sisters, was a multisport athlete, playing several sports, including swimming, hockey, and skiing. In high school, Quinn played varsity volleyball and basketball for all four years. They won MVP honors for basketball and helped lead both teams to conference championships. During their senior year, Quinn won Athlete of the Year for their contributions to both teams. However, their first love was always soccer, which they had begun playing with a club team at the age of six alongside their twin sister, Jillian.

Quinn was a fixture on the Canada Youth National Team scene after being picked for the U14 provincial squad in 2009. They competed on the U17 and U20 teams before making their senior team debut on March 7, 2014, at eighteen years old. Quinn also played at Duke University from 2013 to 2018, where they were named 2017 ACC Midfielder of the Year and a 2017 MAC Hermann Trophy semifinalist, among other athletic and academic accolades in an echo of their high school career.

Quinn studied biology and graduated in 2018, when they immediately joined the National Women's Soccer League, drafted third overall by the Washington Spirit. Quinn has played for Seattle Reign FC since July 2019. A steady midfielder rather than a flashy one, Quinn can be a quiet presence on the field, but don't let that fool you—their savvy field awareness and passing accuracy make their presence felt, if not heard.

Quinn came out as trans nonbinary in September 2020. In their coming-out post on Instagram, Quinn wrote:

> COMING OUT IS HARD. . . . I KNOW FOR ME IT'S SOMETHING I'LL BE DOING OVER AGAIN FOR THE REST OF MY LIFE. AS I'VE LIVED AS AN OPENLY TRANS PERSON WITH THE PEOPLE I LOVE MOST FOR MANY YEARS, I DID ALWAYS WONDER WHEN I'D COME OUT PUBLICLY. . . . I WANT TO BE VISIBLE TO QUEER FOLKS WHO DON'T SEE PEOPLE LIKE THEM ON THEIR FEED. I KNOW IT SAVED MY LIFE YEARS AGO.

Quinn has mentioned soccer as a way to connect with their body in an empowering way, outside of the confines of the gender binary. Quinn hopes that their visibility as an out trans nonbinary professional athlete will demonstrate to trans youth that "they can continue to play the sports they love, and they can also identify as themselves." Quinn continues to advocate for trans rights both in their home country of Canada and in the United States, especially in regard to inclusion in sports. In June 2023 Quinn spoke out against the National Women's Soccer League's problematic transgender athlete policy, urging the league to reconsider the 2021 policy's failure to account for genders that exist outside the binary.

At the Tokyo 2020 Summer Olympics, Quinn made history as one of the first openly trans/nonbinary athletes to compete at the Olympics, appearing in all six of Canada's matches and starting in five of them. Quinn went on to become not only the first trans/nonbinary person to medal but also the first to win Olympic gold. They highlighted the bittersweet nature of this achievement to *The New York Times*:

> I'M IN SUCH A PRIVILEGED POSITION WHERE WE SEE THIS OLYMPICS REALLY HIGHLIGHTING THE DISCRIMINATION OF BLACK WOMEN AS A WHOLE—CIS AND TRANS. ALTHOUGH I, MYSELF, AM WINNING A GOLD MEDAL, THERE ARE SO MANY FOLKS THAT DON'T EVEN HAVE ACCESS TO THE OLYMPICS.
>
> WE'RE NOT EVEN CLOSE TO THE POINT IN SOCIETY WHERE SPORTS ARE ACCESSIBLE TO EVERYONE AND THE OLYMPICS ARE ACCESSIBLE TO EVERYONE. FOR ME, IT'S A LOT OF MIXED FEELINGS TO SEE MYSELF IN THAT POSITION AND ALSO SEE WHERE OTHER COMMUNITIES ARE REALLY STRUGGLING AND BEING FACED WITH A LOT OF DISCRIMINATION.

Quinn was named to the Olympic squad for the third time in 2024, competing in the Paris Summer Olympics. As they continue their activism both on and off the field, Quinn hopes the needle continues to move forward.

LAYSHIA CLARENDON

(THEY / HE / SHE)

- American professional basketball player
- Advocate and activist, including founding the Layshia Clarendon Foundation with Athletes for Impact to broaden healthcare access for trans and nonbinary people
- 2017 WNBA All-Star
- 2018 FIBA Women's Basketball World Cup Gold Medalist (USA)

Did you know? Layshia Clarendon and their spouse had a child in 2020, known publicly as Baby C. He and his wife are practicing a gender-expansive parenting approach in which Baby C is not assigned a gender, allowing Baby C to define it themself as they grow up.

Layshia Clarendon was born on May 2, 1991, in San Bernardino, California, the middle of three children who were constantly competing with one another and the kids in their neighborhood at various sports and made-up games. Clarendon looked up to their sister Jasmine, who is six years older. When Clarendon was in middle school, Jasmine was outed to their parents. Suddenly, being queer was a hot topic in their household, and Clarendon, who'd seen himself reflected in Jasmine's girlfriend, felt himself shrink.

Jasmine went on to play basketball at Pepperdine University, and Clarendon was quickly proving herself to be an elite point guard recruit in the class of 2009. He then played at the University of California, Berkeley, before being selected ninth overall in the 2013 WBNA draft by the Indiana Fever. Clarendon has played for several WNBA teams since their initial three-year stint with the Fever before playing for the Los Angeles Sparks.

Clarendon began speaking more publicly about his queer identity during his senior year at UC Berkeley. A teammate had introduced him to The Way Christian Center, a church with roots in the traditions of Black Pentecostalism that emphasizes an active pursuit of justice. The pastor introduced Clarendon to queer theology, and the faith he found there stays with him to this day, driving much of his own social justice work both within the WBNA and outside it.

When the WNBA launched its first Pride initiative in 2014, much of it felt very underwhelming. Teams were supposed to wear Pride warm-up shirts, but they didn't. The Women's National Basketball Players Association (WNBPA) executive committee had voted

against issuing a leaguewide mandate to wear the shirts. Clarendon advocated to their Fever teammate, who was president of the WNBPA executive committee, about why this was so harmful; the WNBPA mandated that the players would wear the shirts in the next season. That teammate encouraged Clarendon to run for the executive committee, and in 2016 she was elected as first vice president. With the help of this platform, Clarendon would become a driving force for justice in the WNBA.

Clarendon had met her future wife, Jessica Dolan, while at Berkeley, though they didn't start dating until 2015. In 2019, after two years of marriage, Clarendon shared with Dolan that she was questioning her gender. Together, Clarendon and Dolan have navigated Clarendon's journey of self-discovery as transgender and nonbinary—along with parenthood, with their first child born in December 2020.

In May 2020 Clarendon spoke on the podcast *That's What She Said with Sarah Spain*, parsing through, among other topics, their multifaceted coming-out journey to their family.

> IN SOME WAYS, BASKETBALL REALLY SAVED ME AND GAVE ME THE ONLY REALLY SAFE COMMUNITY I HAD GROWING UP, A PLACE TO BE QUEER AND BE OKAY.

As a member of the WNBPA's executive committee, Clarendon helped negotiate the WNBA's new collective bargaining agreement after the 2019 season. Clarendon was the one who, after being elected to a second term, came up with the idea of dedicating the 2020 season to the #SayHerName campaign. Clarendon also led the new social justice council of the WNBPA, hosting webinars with such prominent figures as politician

Stacey Abrams, the Black transgender writer and activist Raquel Willis, and Tamika Palmer—the mother of Breonna Taylor, who was murdered by police officers in her own apartment earlier that same year.

After the 2020 season, Clarendon came out publicly as transgender and nonbinary, becoming the first openly trans nonbinary player in WBNA history. In January 2021, Clarendon underwent top surgery, becoming the first active WNBA player to do so. In a June 2021 cover story with ESPN, Clarendon proclaimed:

> I FEEL VERY WOMAN, AND I FEEL VERY MAN. I FEEL BOTH, AND I FEEL NEITHER, AND I FEEL LIKE ALL THE GENDER EXPANSIVENESS THAT EXISTS IN THE WORLD IS IN ME. I THINK THAT'S WHAT THE WORD TRANS MEANS TO ME, TOO. IT'S SUCH A BEAUTIFUL WORD, AND SUCH A BEAUTIFUL COMMUNITY THAT IS FULL OF RESILIENCE. AND IT . . . IT JUST FEELS LIKE MAGIC.

On September 20, 2024, Clarendon announced their retirement on Instagram. While a bittersweet decision, they told ESPN that "it just felt right. . . . It was just the culmination of my mind, my body, and my spirit telling me that it was time to move on. I just had a deep knowing in my intuition that now is the right time, and I had a really open heart and readiness to let go."

JAIYAH SAELUA

(SHE / HER)

. American Samoan and faʻafafine professional soccer player

Did you know? Jaiyah Saelua is known for wearing full makeup to compete in every match she plays, which makes each crunching defensive tackle a lot of fun to watch.

Jaiyah Saelua was born on July 19, 1988, in Leone, American Samoa. She is a faʻafafine—an Indigenous third gender in Polynesian society so entrenched in the culture of the islands that Saelua never experienced gender discrimination until moving away from home. Saelua also identifies as a transgender woman, but her experience of her gender is tied to her culture.

As a trans woman who comfortably plays as herself on a men's sports team, her experience is very different from that of trans women in Western countries. Saelua describes the faʻafafine identity as a coming-of-age experience, rather than a coming-out moment, within a culture that holds not just space but respect and reverence for such identities. With American Samoa boasting a population of somewhere around sixty thousand people, the majority of whom are Indigenous Samoan, it is no wonder that faʻafafine people continue to be celebrated as an integral part of their culture.

Saelua began playing competitive soccer at age eleven and made her debut for the American Samoa national team just four years later at age fifteen. The American Samoa national soccer team has often been called the worst team in the world, highlighted by their world-record 31–0 loss to Australia in 2001. The team achieved its first FIFA-recognized international win in the 2014 FIFA World Cup qualifiers with a 2–1 win over Tonga in November 2011, a game in which Saelua played a key role as a center-back defender—even notching an assist. Not only did Saelua play a key role as a player, but she also made history as the first transgender and nonbinary person to compete in a FIFA World Cup qualifier.

For Saelua, sport transcends gender—she paused her hormone replacement therapy treatment to give herself a better chance at a comeback after being cut from the national team in 2015. This proved successful, as she went on to captain the team during the 2019 World Cup campaign. Currently, Saelua waffles back and forth between wanting to retire to focus on advocacy work and wanting to play in the 2026 World Cup qualifiers and 2027 Pacific Games.

Saelua has been portrayed in film twice. First, she was featured in the 2014 documentary *Next Goal Wins*, which chronicles the American Samoa team's efforts to qualify for the 2014 World Cup. A fictionalized version of the documentary, also titled *Next Goal Wins*, from director Taika Waititi was released in 2023, in which Saelua is portrayed by fa'afafine actor Kaimana. On the portrayal of her story in the film, Saelua told *Vanity Fair*:

> IT'S IMPORTANT THAT THESE UNCOMFORTABLE SITUATIONS THAT TRANS PEOPLE AND LGBTQIA+ PEOPLE ACTUALLY GO THROUGH ARE VISIBLE.

Waititi's version focuses more on the journey of the coach than that of the players, with the character of Thomas Rongen misgendering and deadnaming Saelua several times to show his journey from villain to hero. In reality? Rongen immediately noticed that Saelua's teammates were calling her a different name than the one on the roster, at which point he walked right up to her and asked what she wanted to be called.

We should all be so lucky to be embraced without question. Hopefully, someday, we will be.

POLITICS

DR. AMITA KUTTNER

(THEY / THEM)

- Canadian astrophysicist, scientist, politician, and environmental advocate
- Cofounder and copresident of moonlight · institute, a nonprofit that aims to "nurture a sustainable framework for an equitable and just future" in addressing the climate crisis

Did you know? Amita Kuttner is also a musician and artist. As they wrote on their website, "I write, paint, and sing, though I am waiting for my voice to settle on testosterone to get back into choir and opera."

Amita Kuttner was born on December 4, 1990, in North Vancouver, the child of immigrants—their father was born in London and their mother in Hong Kong. Kuttner was fascinated by the universe and natural world from an early age and still feels happiest with their hands in the earth.

In January 2005, while fourteen-year-old Kuttner was away at boarding school in California a devastating mudslide crashed into their home from the Seymour River, killing their mother and permanently saddling their father with brain damage and other physical injuries. Kuttner has spoken candidly not only about this tragedy but also about their later diagnosis of post-traumatic stress disorder in the wake of their struggles to come to terms with it.

Another result of this tragedy? A commitment to climate justice that would eventually move beyond the classroom and into the political sphere.

Kuttner attended the University of California, Santa Cruz, earning a PhD in astronomy and astrophysics. While their research focused on such phenomena as black holes, wormholes, and quantum effects, they continued to grow increasingly concerned about the rising prevalence of natural disasters like flooding and wildfires, both in their native British Columbia and around the world.

After the 2016 election of Donald Trump to the US presidency, Kuttner felt they could no longer stand by, and in the 2019 Canadian federal election Kuttner ran as a Green Party candidate for a seat in Canada's House of Commons (the same year they successfully defended their thesis).

It was during this electoral campaign that Kuttner decided to come out publicly as nonbinary, transgender, genderfluid, and pansexual. In an interview with *The Tyee*, Kuttner said:

Kuttner's platform centered a scientific approach to social justice, calling for electoral reform, climate action, gender-inclusive policy, and the protection of workers' rights in combination with AI regulation.

While Kuttner ended their 2019 electoral campaign in fourth place, they continued to serve as the Green Party of Canada's Science and Innovation critic until February 2020. Kuttner ran for leadership of the Green Party in 2020 and served as the interim leader from November 2021 until November 2022, where they worked to address systemic inequities within the party and to rebuild unification during a time of "transition and renewal." With this appointment to interim leader, Kuttner became the first openly trans/nonbinary person, the first person of East Asian heritage, and, at age thirty, the youngest person to ever lead a federal political party in Canada.

Since leaving office, Kuttner has continued to work with their nonprofit, the moonlight · institute, as copresident in their quest to a more just and equitable world.

HON. UZOMA ASAGWARA

(THEY / THEM)

. Canadian politician, activist, and psychiatric nurse

- o Deputy Premier of Manitoba (2023–)
- o Manitoba Minister of Health, Seniors and Long-Term Care (2023–)
- o Member of the Legislative Assembly of Manitoba (Union Station) (2019–)

Did you know? Before entering politics, Uzoma Asagwara played for the Canada Women's National Basketball Team for two years, during which they played in the 2007 Pan American Games.

Uzoma Asagwara was born on September 23, 1984, in Winnipeg, Manitoba, to Igbo Nigerian parents who immigrated to Canada in the late 1970s. Asagwara's parents highlighted the importance of community involvement through their work with local organizations and community groups, instilling that same passion for advocacy in their five children.

In the spirit of that passion—and while playing basketball at the University of Winnipeg and on the Canada Women's National Team—Asagwara studied psychiatric nursing in a joint program between the University of Winnipeg and Brandon University, graduating in 2008. Asagwara then worked as a registered psychiatric nurse for more than a decade, specializing in addictions and acute mental health for both youth and adults.

They also continued their work as a community activist, founding Queer People of Colour Winnipeg in 2014 to both create safe spaces for and promote the rights of queer and gender-diverse Black, Indigenous, and people of color in the city. About this work, Asagwara said to *PUNCH*:

Asagwara's work in public service as a psychiatric nurse, along with their community activism, inspired a move into local politics. Asagwara served as a member of the Premier's Advisory Council on Education, Poverty, and Citizenship before making their own bid for office, running on a platform of accessibility to health care, affordable housing, and quality education.

On their work, Asagwara told The Green Institute:

WHEN WE ENSURE THAT THERE ARE NO BARRIERS IN THE WAY OF ANYBODY ACCESSING THE SERVICES THAT THEY NEED, WHEN WE TAKE CARE OF THOSE IN OUR COMMUNITIES WHO ARE MOST VULNERABLE, IT BENEFITS, ABSOLUTELY, EVERYBODY.

In September 2019, Asagwara was sworn in as one of the first three Black Canadians, the first queer Black person, and the first nonbinary person ever elected to the Legislative Assembly of Manitoba. In this capacity, Asagwara successfully passed a bill to recognize Somali Heritage Week. They also served as the official opposition critic for health and introduced bills in support of trans and nonbinary people, such as a bill to allow for gender-neutral government-issued identification.

Asagwara was reelected for a second term with the New Democratic Party in October 2023, making further history when they were also appointed the eleventh deputy premier of Manitoba under incoming premier Wab Kinew. In this role, Asagwara continues their work on behalf of marginalized communities in Manitoba.

MAEBE A. GIRL

(SHE / THEY)

- American drag queen and politician
- Silver Lake Neighborhood councilwoman

Did you know? One of Maebe A. Girl's first jobs was leading pizza tours of Chicago. Now you know who to ask for the best pizza!

Maebe A. Girl was born in Pittsburgh, Pennsylvania, on July 27, 1986. When she was nine years old, her family moved to the Chicago area, where she remained through her late twenties before moving to Los Angeles in 2014. Although Girl came out to their parents at age sixteen, they didn't start living more authentically until moving to LA and beginning their drag career.

Girl's first taste of politics came in Chicago when she considered running for mayor in 2011 but was unable to get on the ballot after failing to get the required number of signatures. "Starting drag brought me back into politics," Girl told the *Chicago Sun-Times*. "Just the mere act of going out and performing in drag is a political and social statement." Girl takes that one step further as a drag queen—she first became known for her satirical impressions of political figures like Melania Trump, Betsy DeVos, Kellyanne Conway, and Sarah Huckabee Sanders.

In 2019 Girl took another step straight into politics itself, when she declared a run for the Silver Lake Neighborhood Council on a platform of uplifting LGBTQIA+ rights, addressing the homelessness crisis, and protecting immigrants.

On April 16, 2019, Girl became the first trans person to be elected to a municipal position. That June, Girl declared their intent to challenge incumbent Adam Schiff in the March 2020 primary election for California's Twenty-eighth Congressional District, coming in third overall.

In her second campaign against twenty-two-year incumbent Schiff in 2022 (though in the restructured Thirtieth Congressional District), she finished second out of nine candidates and progressed to the general election, where she stunned and impressed by winning nearly 30 percent of the votes cast—more than 60,000 of approximately 211,000 votes.

In doing so, Girl became the first trans nonbinary person ever to advance to a general election for a seat in Congress—and the first drag queen to do so.

With six-inch heels, a sleek blond bob, and brightly colored power suits, Girl is a force to be reckoned with and one who refuses to be ignored. Though the tabloids have put much emphasis on her being a drag queen, Girl herself emphasizes her transness: "Drag is what I do, trans is who I am." She also said to KCRW:

Girl made their third run for Congress in the March 2024 primary election but did not advance to the general election. She continues to serve as treasurer and at-large representative on the Silver Lake Neighborhood Council. She also hosts the Wigs & Waffles drag brunch.

DRAG IS ACTUALLY A PART OF HOW I EXPRESS MY GENDER IDENTITY . . . I FEEL LIKE BOTH A BOY AND A GIRL, SOMETIMES A LITTLE BIT MORE BOY, SOMETIMES A LITTLE BIT MORE GIRL. HENCE MY NAME ACTUALLY REALLY DOES MAKE SENSE.

AUDREY TANG

(PRONOUNS: ANY)

. Taiwanese politician and free software programmer
. First Minister of Digital Affairs of Taiwan (2022–2024)

Did you know? Audrey Tang was a consultant and digital advisor to Apple from 2010 to 2016 and helped develop the company's virtual assistant, Siri.

Audrey Tang was born in Taipei, Taiwan, on April 18, 1981, and swiftly became known as a child prodigy. Due to a congenital heart condition, Tang was required to stay as relaxed and still as possible, which made it so that she struggled to connect with her peers. From a very young age, Tang was an avid reader of classical literature and nonfiction such as advanced mathematics. Tang started learning how to code and program by age eight, teaching himself programming languages like Haskell and Perl.

Tang dropped out of school at age fourteen and started a search engine company at fifteen, becoming immersed in the beginnings of the World Wide Web. Tang worked as a digital consultant through the 1990s and 2000s and soon became known as a free software programmer (also known as a civic hacker or hacktivist), though it wasn't until 2014 that he made a name for himself beyond the tech sphere.

In March 2014, student protesters in Taiwan set off a chain reaction of citizen activism. They temporarily seized control of the national legislature, occupying the parliament building for around three weeks in opposition to a pending free trade agreement with China. The protesters received massive support around Taiwan for what came to be known as the Sunflower Movement. A catalyst for further student and civic activism, the Sunflower Movement led to the Democratic Progressive Party of Taiwan coming to power in the January 2016 election.

But how did this movement become so widely known? With the help of hacktivists like Audrey Tang, who set up improvised broadband connections to broadcast the movement's protests and debates to the outside world in real time. The Taiwanese government, rather than prosecute Tang for their role in broadcasting the Sunflower Movement, offered them a job in designing a media literacy curriculum for schools in Taiwan. In 2016 Tang was appointed minister without portfolio of digital affairs, becoming the youngest and the first openly transgender and nonbinary cabinet member in Taiwan's history.

The Ministry of Digital Affairs (moda) was not established as a full cabinet-level ministry until August 2022, with Tang as the inaugural minister. The ministry combines digital innovation with emocracy in order to create sustainable digital initiatives across industries and infrastructure, from economics to health care.

Taiwan had arguably the most successful response to the onset of the coronavirus pandemic in 2020. Tang is credited with "hacking" the coronavirus, launching a series of "mask maps" to prevent hoarding and spearheading digital initiatives to combat disinformation. A conservative anarchist, Tang believes strongly in radical transparency and advocates for open-source approaches to both technology and democracy.

While serving as minister of digital affairs from August 27, 2022, to May 20, 2024, Tang recorded, transcribed, and uploaded every moda meeting online in the interest of transparency and continually highlighted the need for civic participation, creating various avenues by which citizens might weigh in on various issues (for example, AI and how it might be regulated in order to enhance democracy rather than denigrate it).

Tang continues to support democratic innovation by contributing to g0v, the decentralized civic hacking community that they helped program back in 2014, and by serving on the board of nonprofit organization RadicalxChange. On their identity, Tang told the podcast *Art of Power*:

> I AM LITERALLY NONBINARY, AND NOT JUST IN GENDER.

Tang initially came out as a transgender woman, beginning their transition in 2005. Tang most recently identifies as transgender, nonbinary, and postgender. They highlight the word *nonbinary* as not just their gender but as a metaphor for their ideology and way of life.

ACTIVISTS & SCHOLARS

DR. JAMES MAKOKIS

(HE / HIM)

- Nehiyô two-spirit (Plains Cree)
- Family physician, clinical professor, and medical director
- 2007 Indspire Award Laureate—Youth
- 2019 Distinguished Alumni Award, MacEwan University
- 2020 Alumni Award of Distinction—Rising Star Achievement Award, Faculty of Medicine, University of Ottawa

Did you know? James Makokis is an avid marathon runner. He and his husband, Anthony Johnson, won season 7 of *The Amazing Race Canada* in 2019, competing as Team Ahkameyimok, which loosely means "never give up" in the Plains Cree language.

Dr. James Makokis was born in the early 1980s and grew up in the Saddle Lake Cree Nation in Treaty 6 territory, in what is now known as northeastern Alberta, Canada. At age seventeen, Makokis came out as gay. While his mother, Patricia, a former president of Blue Quills First Nations College (now University nuhelot'įne thaiyots'į nistameyimâkanak Blue Quills), supported him immediately, his father struggled to come to terms with his sexuality at first. Through community support, they found a way together. Makokis now also identifies as two-spirit. On his identity, Makokis told nonprofit Cultural Survival:

TWO-SPIRIT IS A CONTEMPORARY ENGLISH TERM TO REFLECT GENDER DIVERSITY THAT INDIGENOUS NATIONS HAVE ALWAYS HAD. . . . A LOT OF THOSE TEACHINGS OF GENDER DIVERSITY HAVE BEEN LOST, AND A LOT OF PEOPLE ARE SEARCHING FOR THEIR IDENTITY AS TWO-SPIRIT PEOPLE AND THE ROLES AND RESPONSIBILITIES THAT COME WITH THAT.

Makokis first knew he wanted to be a doctor by the time he was three or four years old. He graduated from the University of Toronto with a master's in health science in 2006 before going on to attend medical school at the University of Ottawa, graduating in 2010. Makokis also completed the Aboriginal family medicine residency program at the University of British Columbia in 2012.

As a family physician, Makokis is an internationally recognized leader in the areas of Indigenous and transgender health, with trans patients coming from around the world to seek his treatments. His work seeks to reclaim and revitalize these practices in order to best support his patients.

Makokis approaches patients first as a Nehiyô two-spirit person and second as a doctor, with his clinical practices rooted in the Cree Natural Law of kindness, honesty, strength, determination, and sharing as taught to him by his Elders. He incorporates traditional Indigenous medicine as well as Western diagnostic tools into patient care.

As an Indigenous, two-spirit, and gay person, Makokis understands firsthand the discrimination and racism that both Indigenous and 2SLGBTQIA+ people face within the health care system. He advocates for the inclusion of both Indigenous health care and trans health care as core issues within curriculums in order to better educate upcoming doctors and to recognize Indigenous health care and trans health care as legitimate among medical institutions.

Makokis continues to champion the right of Indigenous Peoples to traditional Indigenous medicine as well as the right of trans people to gender-affirming health care.

DR. JONATHAN P. HIGGINS

(THEY / THEM)

- American educator, professor, national speaker, cultural critic, entertainment analyst, freelance journalist, thought leader
- 2015 National Black Justice Coalition Emerging Leaders to Watch
- 2017 Lambda Literary Fellow—Nonfiction
- 2021 Culture Strike Disruptors Fellow
- 2021 guest baker on the Netflix series *Nailed It!*

Did you know? Dr. Jonathan P. Higgins counts writer Audre Lorde and trans icon Marsha P. Johnson among their inspirations.

Dr. Jonathan P. Higgins was born on July 29, 1985, and raised in San Bernardino, California. When they were about five years old, their parents separated and divorced. Only after Higgins turned ten did their father attempt to reconnect with them and their brother, but it was sporadic, and for all intents and purposes, they were raised in poverty by a single mother.

They were also raised as a Jehovah's Witness. Throughout childhood and adolescence, Higgins struggled with the dissonance between the organization's focus on "what a man *should* be" (e.g., hypermasculine, patriarchal, stoic) and their own diverging interests in pop culture, performance, and dance, especially the likes of Destiny's Child and Beyoncé. While Higgins always knew they were "different," it wasn't until they attended college at California State University, San Bernardino (CSUSB),

that they began to come to terms with their identity, even as they battled depression over what it would mean to leave Jehovah's Witnesses. Higgins finally broke away from the organization in 2004.

Higgins studied communication studies and women's studies at CSUSB before going on to graduate school at the University of Redlands, where they earned both a master of arts in management and a doctorate in educational leadership in social justice. Their dissertation, which they successfully defended in 2015, examined the experiences of queer men of color in higher education. Since then, Higgins has continued their work in social justice, serving as a consultant on inclusion projects for brands such as Amazon Prime, Apple, Disney, Fox, Instagram, the NFL, and Ulta Beauty. Higgins has also consulted with several universities and has been a professor at the University of Redlands since 2019.

As a writer and speaker, Higgins continues to examine the intersections of identity, gender, and race in media and what liberation means for marginalized individuals, while advocating for more visibility and representation of marginalized people in media.

In 2017 they gave their first TEDx Talk, "From Fear to Freedom," on embracing personal power and freedom through unlearning fear. In an October 2018 piece for *Slate*, they wrote:

THROUGH MUCH SELF-EXAMINATION AND THERAPY, I CAME UPON THE WORD NONBINARY AS A TOOL TO HELP ME TO FIND MY PLACE IN GENDER AND TO FIGHT BACK AGAINST THE EXPECTATIONS THAT WERE PLACED ON ME AS A BLACK MALE. I BEGAN TO SEE THIS WORD AND ITS DEFINITION AS A WAY TO NOT ONLY UNDERSTAND MY EXPERIENCE IN THE WORLD, BUT FOR ME TO RECLAIM MY IDENTITY. AS THE YEARS PROGRESSED, I HAVE COME TO UNDERSTAND WHY MY EXISTENCE AS A BLACK, QUEER, NONBINARY PERSON IS NOT ONLY POWERFUL, BUT RADICAL. BY OWNING BOTH MY MASCULINITY AND MY FEMININITY, I HAVE BEEN ABLE TO REDEFINE WHAT FREEDOM LOOKS LIKE BEYOND CERTAIN LIMITING GENDER NORMS WITHIN BLACK CULTURE.

Since 2021, Higgins has been the creator, host, and executive producer of the Shorty Award–winning *BFF: Black, Fat, Femme* podcast through iHeartMedia, which celebrates all intersections of identity. Higgins serves as the director of media relations and advocacy at the Rainbow Pride Youth Alliance. Their debut book is titled *Black. Fat. Femme: Revealing the Power of Visibly Queer Voices in Media and Learning to Love Yourself.*

DR. JUDITH BUTLER

(THEY / THEM)

- American philosopher, human rights activist, critical theorist, gender studies scholar, and author
- Distinguished Professor at the Graduate School at University of California, Berkeley
- Hannah Arendt Chair at the European Graduate School
- 1979 Fulbright Scholar
- 1998 Guggenheim Fellow
- 2001 David R. Kessler Award, CLAGS: The Center for LGBTQ Studies
- 2007 American Philosophical Society electee
- 2008 Andrew W. Mellon Foundation Distinguished Achievement Award
- 2012 Theodor W. Adorno Prize
- 2015 Corresponding Fellow of the British Academy
- 2019 American Academy of Arts and Sciences Fellow
- 2022 Catalonia International Prize

Did you know? When Judith Butler was twelve years old, they considered two possible career paths: philosopher or clown.

D r. Judith Butler was born in Cleveland, Ohio, on February 24, 1956, to a dentist father and a mother who worked in fair housing and helped run Ohio Democrats political campaigns. The middle child of three, Butler said to *The New Yorker* that their siblings "monopolized the genders—he was Mr. Man, and she was this petite dancer who went to Juilliard. I was—I don't know." Butler was raised in Reform Judaism. From age fourteen, they attended Hebrew school and special classes on Jewish ethics, which they consider their "first training in philosophy." Around the same time, their family discovered that both Butler and two cousins were gay, and all three were shamed for it and suffered. Even still, Butler said, "We were the queer revenge. We're not going to conform to everybody's idea of what we should be."

Butler graduated from Yale University after transferring from Bennington College, earning a bachelor of arts in philosophy in 1978 and a doctorate of philosophy in 1984. While their first book was published in 1987, it was their 1988 essay, "Performative Acts and Gender Constitution," and their 1990 publication, *Gender Trouble: Feminism and the Subversion of Identity*, that spearheaded their catapult into the forefront of critical theory.

Gender Trouble introduced the idea of gender as something we *do* as a cultural activity rather than something we *are*. Butler has continued to explore and refine their theory of gender performativity (or a social construction of gender) over the years, most notably in *Bodies That Matter: On the Discursive Limits of "Sex"* (1993) and *Undoing Gender* (2004). *Gender Trouble* remains a foundational text in gender studies and feminist scholarship, even as discussions of gender have moved ever further in-between and beyond the binary. Butler told *The New York Times*:

> AT THE TIME THAT I WROTE GENDER TROUBLE, I CALLED FOR A WORLD IN WHICH WE MIGHT THINK ABOUT GENDERS BEING PROLIFERATED BEYOND THE USUAL BINARY OF MAN AND WOMAN. WHAT WOULD THAT LOOK LIKE? WHAT WOULD IT BE? SO WHEN PEOPLE STARTED TALKING ABOUT BEING "NONBINARY," I THOUGHT, WELL, I AM THAT. I WAS TRYING TO OCCUPY THAT SPACE OF BEING BETWEEN EXISTING CATEGORIES.

Butler's work has also delved into other areas of political oppression, social justice, and the dehumanization of marginalized peoples. They highlight the concept of mourning as a political act, summarized by what they call "grievable life," in which some lives are rarely individually or publicly acknowledged when lost. Butler has pointed out specific communities where individuals primarily go unnamed and therefore erased in media publications when lost, such as AIDS victims, prisoners in Guantanamo Bay, refugees crossing borders, Palestinians killed by the Israeli military, and Black people killed by police in the United States. Butler's idea of a "radical equality of grievability," in turn, would mean that all lives are seen as equally valuable and so are equally grieved when lost.

Butler considers themself anti-war and is a proponent of nonviolence, supported by their own activism on behalf of movements such as Occupy Wall Street and Black Lives Matter. Butler has served as a member of the advisory board of Jewish Voice for Peace since 2016. On trans-exclusionary radical feminism, Butler said to *The New Statesman* that it is "a fringe movement that is seeking to speak in the name of the mainstream, and that our responsibility is to refuse to let that happen." Butler's 2024 book, *Who's Afraid of Gender?*, further explores the idea and history of the "anti-gender ideology movement," which Butler explains should be considered "a neo-fascist phenomenon." This work continues to explore the ways in which gender is both enforced and resisted.

Butler is a lesbian and legally nonbinary. They have taught at Berkeley since 1993, where they live with their partner, political theorist Wendy Brown. Their son, Isaac, a musician, lives nearby.

69

GLOSSARY

In creating this guide, we referenced resources from organizations like the Trevor Project, GLAAD, Gender Spectrum, the Human Rights Campaign, GLSEN, and PFLAG. If you have questions about gender, these resources are a great place to start.

Agender refers to someone who does not identify with or experience any gender.

Bigender refers to someone whose gender identity encompasses two genders (often man and woman, but not exclusively) or is moving between being two genders.

Cisgender refers to someone whose gender identity aligns with the gender they were assigned at birth.

BIPOC stands for Black, Indigenous, People of Color.

Cisnormativity is the assumption that everyone is cisgender and that being cisgender is superior to all other genders. This includes the often implicitly held idea that being cisgender is the norm and that other genders are "different" or "abnormal."

Demigender refers to someone whose gender identity is only partly male (demiboy) or partly female (demigirl), regardless of their assigned gender at birth.

Faʻafafine and **faʻafatama** are Indigenous third and fourth genders in Polynesian society on the island of Samoa. **Faʻafafine**, translated as "in the manner of a woman," refers to someone assigned male at birth, while **faʻafatama**, translated as "in the manner of a man," refers to someone assigned female at birth. Faʻafafine and faʻafatama people move fluidly between and even transcend male and female roles. They hold highly respected, integral places in society, often taking on caregiver roles for elders and serving as educators to the community on topics considered taboo for men and women to speak of in public conversation.

Gender describes the internal experience of being a **man**, a **woman**, a **nonbinary person**, or otherwise. Every person experiences gender differently, and you cannot know someone's gender simply by looking at them. There are multiple facets of gender, such as gender expression.

Gender diversity refers to the infinite realm of possible gender identities, experiences, or expressions.

Genderfluid describes a person who does not identify with a single fixed gender and/or someone whose gender is dynamic and changing rather than static. Genderfluid people might move between multiple genders.

Genderqueer describes a person who doesn't identify with and often rejects conventional gender identities, roles, expression, or expectations. *Genderqueer* can be an umbrella term for people who blur preconceived boundaries of gender in relation to the gender binary, but it can also be a nonbinary identification.

The **gender binary** is a disproven system that constructs gender according to two discrete and opposite categories—boy/man and girl/woman—and therefore everyone must be one or the other. It's often misused to assert that gender is biologically determined, reinforcing the misconception that men and women are "opposites" with naturally differing roles in society.

Gender dysphoria is the distress experienced when a person's gender identity does not align with what they were assigned at birth and/or with how their gender presents to others. Not everyone experiences gender dysphoria, and for those who do, they might not experience it all the time.

Gender euphoria is the thrill experienced when others recognize and respect one's gender, when one's body aligns with one's gender, and/or when one expresses themself in accordance with their gender.

Gender expression describes the way in which people present or express their gender to others through external means such as physical appearance, clothing, hairstyle, voice, and mannerisms. While most people's understandings of gender expressions relate to their cultural interpretations of masculinity and femininity, there are countless combinations that may incorporate both stereotypically masculine and feminine expressions or neither. All people have gender expressions, and gender expression does not always correlate to gender identity.

Gender identity describes a person's deeply held internal sense of self in relation to their gender, whether masculine, feminine, a blend of both, neither, or something else entirely. Gender identity can either correspond to or differ in varying degrees from one's assigned gender at birth. A person can have an awareness of their gender as early as eighteen months old but might come to an understanding of their gender later in life. The language a person uses to communicate their gender identity can evolve and shift over time, especially as someone gains access to a broader gender vocabulary.

Gender roles refer to the set of societal beliefs that dictate the so-called acceptable behaviors for people of different genders, usually binary in nature. Many people find these restrictive and harmful as they reinforce the gender binary.

Gender spectrum refers to the concept that gender exists beyond a simple man/woman binary model and instead exists on a continuum. Some people fall toward more masculine or feminine aspects, some people move fluidly along the spectrum, and some exist off the spectrum entirely.

Neopronouns are pronouns created to be gender-neutral or without gender, such as *xe/xem, ze/zir,* or *fae/faer.* Contrary to popular belief, this is not a twenty-first-century phenomenon: the idea of creating additional gender-neutral pronouns (sometimes called epicene pronouns) has been documented as early as 1850.

Nonbinary refers to someone whose gender identity exists between, beyond, and/or outside the gender binary categories of male and female. For nonbinary people, their gender might be both male and female, neither, somewhere in-between, or something else entirely. *Nonbinary* can also be used as an umbrella term encompassing identities such as agender, bigender, genderqueer, or genderfluid. Some nonbinary people might consider their own identity as falling under the transgender umbrella or might use additional descriptors to delineate the specific way in which they are nonbinary.

Transfeminine refers to people who were assigned male at birth and identify more with femininity. This can include trans women, nonbinary people, and other gender-diverse identities.

Transgender refers to people whose gender identity differs from what they were assigned at birth.

Transmasculine refers to people who were assigned female at birth and identify more with masculinity. This can include trans men, nonbinary people, and other gender-diverse identities.

Two-spirit is an umbrella term created by First Nations/Native American/Indigenous peoples to describe a sexual orientation and/or gender/sex that exists outside colonial constructions of the gender binary (neither man nor woman but a distinct alternative gender status exclusive to their ethnicity). This term should not be appropriated by or used to describe people who are not First Nations/Native American/ Indigenous.

REFERENCED MEDIA

Can't remember all the gender-expansive and gender-inclusive media we mentioned throughout this book? Here's a list of some of them:

FILM & TV

- *She-Ra and the Princesses of Power*, Netflix
- *Nimona*, Netflix
- *The Owl House*, Disney Channel
- *Adventure Time*, Cartoon Network
- *Steven Universe*, Cartoon Network

BOOKS, COMICS & GRAPHIC NOVELS

- *Lumberjanes* by ND Stevenson
- *Nimona* by ND Stevenson
- *The Witch Boy* by Molly Knox Ostertag
- *The Girl from the Sea* by Molly Knox Ostertag
- *Bianca Torre Is Afraid of Everything* by Justine Pucella Winans
- *The Wicked Bargain* by Gabe Cole Novoa
- *Transmogrify!: 14 Fantastical Tales of Trans Magic*, edited by g. haron davis
- *Venom & Vow* by Anna-Marie McLemore and Elliott McLemore
- *Gender Queer: A Memoir* by Maia Kobabe
- *When We Were Magic* by Sarah Gailey

DISCOVER MORE

There are so many incredible and influential **nonbinary**, **genderqueer**, and **otherwise gender-diverse** people around the world who couldn't fit into this book. Here are more amazing communities you can learn about:

On Two-Spirit Identities

Human Rights Campaign Foundation. "Two Spirit and LGBTQ+ Identities: Today and Centuries Ago." November 23, 2020. hrc.org/news/two-spirit-and-lgbtq-idenitites-today-and-centuries-ago.

Human Rights Campaign Foundation and American Indian College Fund. "Understanding Native LGBTQ+ Identities." Accessed August 13, 2024. hrc.org/resources/understanding -native-lgbtq-identities.

Montiel, Anya. "LGBTQIA+ Pride and Two-Spirit People." Smithsonian.com. June 23, 2021. smithsonianmag.com/blogs/national-museum-american-indian/2021/06/23/lgbtqia-pride -and-two-spirit-people/.

On Samoan Queer Lives

McMullin, Dan Taulapapa, and Yuki Kihara. *Somoan Queer Lives.* Little Island Press, 2018.

National History Museum. "Beyond Gender: Indigenous Perspectives, Fa'afafine and Fa'afatama." September 1, 2020. nhm.org/stories/beyond-gender-indigenous-perspectives-faafafine-and -faafatama.

On Other Specific Indigenous Identities

Yazzie, Jolene. "Why are Diné LGBTQ+ and Two Spirit people being denied access to ceremony?" *High Country News*, January 7, 2020. hcn.org/issues/52-2/indigenous-affairs-why-are-dine -lgbtq-and-two-spirit-people-being-denied-access-to-ceremony/.

National History Museum. "Beyond Gender: Indigenous Perspectives, Mapuche." September 15, 2020. nhm.org/stories/beyond-gender-indigenous-perspectives-mapuche.

National History Museum. "Beyond Gender: Indigenous Perspectives, Muxe." September 15, 2020. nhm.org/stories/beyond-gender-indigenous-perspectives-muxe.

ABOUT THE AUTHOR

em dickson (*e/em/eir/she*) is a school librarian, authenticity reader, competitive sailor, and sea shanty enthusiast with a dual MA/MFA in children's literature/writing for children and young adults from Simmons University. Like Peter Pan, e has a strong emotional attachment to eir shadow, a fluffy black muppet of a dog called Luna, who may or may not be a selkie. When not reading or writing, e can be found harmonizing to random sounds, collecting trinkets in eir pockets like a dragon, or promoting the color teal. Someday e will have a home library with a secret door and a friendly ghost. E feels most at home by the sea, which is convenient since e spends most of eir time in coastal Massachusetts. You can find em across social media platforms as @mlereads.

ABOUT THE ILLUSTRATOR

Cameron Mukwa (*he/him*) is an illustrator and graphic novelist. He shares his Anishinaabe heritage through storytelling and pattern design, focusing on stories that center his lived experience as a nonbinary, transgender, and two-spirit person. He loves bright colors and bold designs, illustrating representation for people of all backgrounds, and showing kids of all ages that it's good to be different. Common themes in his work are transgender life, gender euphoria, urban fantasy, and Indigenous narrative.

His debut graphic novel, *The Ribbon Skirt*, was published in November 2024. He is also a sought-after artist for educational publishers.

Cameron uses both traditional and digital media to create his work. His ideal projects would include illustrations that illuminate the LGBTQ+ and BIPOC experiences, symbolic works of fantasy or science fiction, or explorations of established properties from a non-white, non-straight perspective.

See more of Cameron's work at cameronmukwa.com.

Andrews McMeel Publishing
a division of Andrews McMeel Universal
1130 Walnut Street, Kansas City, Missouri 64106

www.andrewsmcmeel.com

25 26 27 28 29 TEN 10 9 8 7 6 5 4 3 2 1

ISBN: 978-1-5248-9399-6

Library of Congress Control Number: 2024944182

Editor: Cindy Harris
Art Director: Tiffany Meairs
Production Editor: Kayla Overbey
Production Manager: Jeff Preuss

ATTENTION: SCHOOLS AND BUSINESSES
Andrews McMeel books are available at quantity discounts with bulk purchase for educational, business, or sales promotional use. For information, please e-mail the Andrews McMeel Publishing Special Sales Department: sales@andrewsmcmeel.com.